THE MAYA

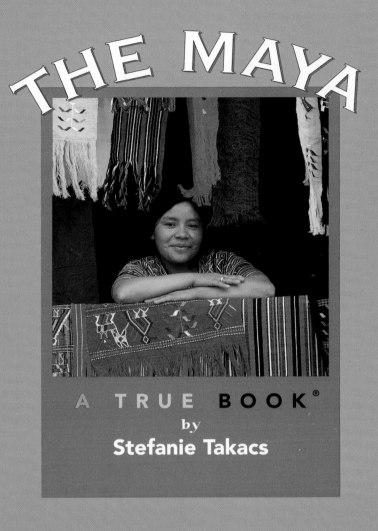

A TRUE BOOK®

by
Stefanie Takacs

Children's Press®
A Division of Scholastic Inc.

New York Toronto London Auckland Sydney
Mexico City New Delhi Hong Kong
Danbury, Connecticut

A Maya family with their prize cabbages

Reading Consultant
Jeanne Clidas, Ph.D.
*National Reading Consultant
and Professor of Reading,
SUNY Brockport*

Content Consultant
Phil Wanyerka
*Department of Anthropology
Cleveland State University*

Library of Congress Cataloging-in-Publication Data

Takacs, Stefanie.
    The Maya / by Stefanie Takacs.— 1st American ed.
        p. cm. — (A true book)
    Includes bibliographical references and index.
    ISBN 0-516-22778-5 (lib. bdg.)   0-516-27907-6 (pbk.)
    1. Mayas—Juvenile literature. [1. Mayas. 2. Indians of Central
America.] I. Title. II. Series.
F1435.T335 2003
972.81'016—dc21

2003004541

1 2 3 4 5 6 7 8 9 10 R 12 11 10 09 08 07 06 05 04 03

Contents

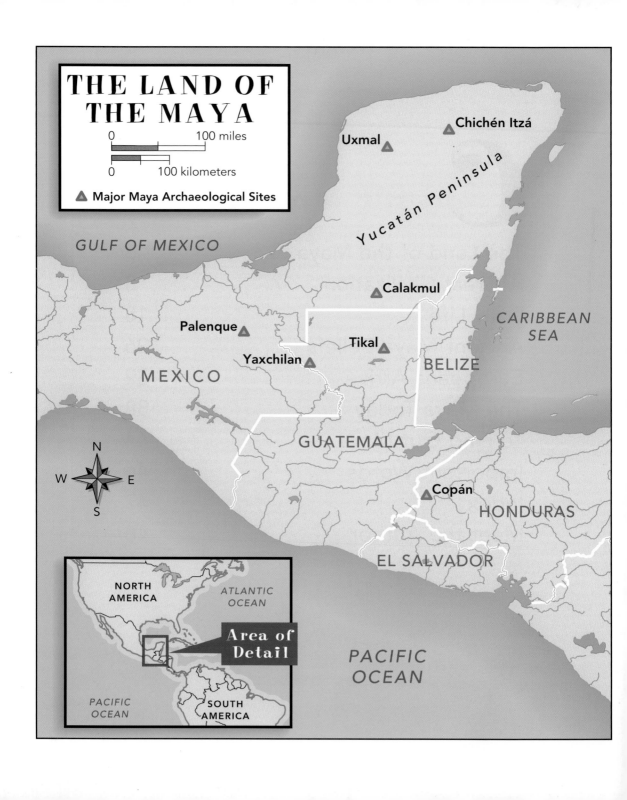

The Land of the Maya

About three thousand years ago, people settled in what we now call Central America. They built their villages in the rain forests of the Yucatán (YU-cah-tan) Peninsula. These people came to be called the Maya (MY-ya).

In the rain forest were ceiba (SAY-ba) trees and other jungle plants. Many animals lived there, including monkeys, hummingbirds, parrots, turkeys, deer, and several kinds of wild cats. The Maya thought the jaguar was the most important animal of all. They believed it was a god because it was the most powerful animal in the forest.

Over time, Maya settlements spread beyond the rain forest to the drier lowlands of the north and the highland areas to the south. Eventually, the

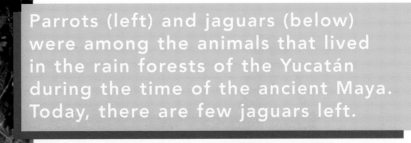

Parrots (left) and jaguars (below) were among the animals that lived in the rain forests of the Yucatán during the time of the ancient Maya. Today, there are few jaguars left.

land of the Maya included parts of present-day southern Mexico, Belize, Guatemala, Honduras, and El Salvador.

A Great Civilization

The Maya **culture** was at its peak from about A.D. 250 to 900. During this time, the Maya accomplished many things. Some historians say the Maya were the most advanced people in this region of the world at the time.

Each Maya city had its own king. Most of the Maya were

The Maya built observatories, such as this one at Chichén Itzá, to help them study the night sky and the path of the sun.

farmers and laborers who worked hard for their king. The Maya king also had many priests, mathematicians, and **astronomers** who worked for him. They spent their time studying the movements of the stars, the moon, and the sun. They used what they learned to make calendars and accurate predictions about the seasons. Like our modern calendar, the Maya solar calendar included 365 days.

The Maya was the only culture in the Americas that developed a system of writing. They wrote with pictures we call *hieroglyphs* (HI-row-glifs). Maya scribes, or writers, wrote many hieroglyphic books. The Maya also had a number system based on the number twenty. They commonly used three

The ancient Maya used hieroglyphs to record events (left). This page from a Maya book (right) includes some Maya numbers. The red symbol in the middle stands for the number thirteen.

symbols: a dot (for the number 1), a bar (for the number 5), and a shell-like shape (for the number 0). The Maya used these symbols to record dates, sometimes millions of years in the past or future.

An ancient Maya carving showing a warrior presenting captured enemies to his king

The kings of different Maya cities were often at war with each other. It was important not to kill one's enemies in battle, though. The Maya captured their enemies and brought them back to their cities. Then they

sacrificed the enemies to the gods during religious ceremonies. Warriors who captured many enemies were highly respected in Maya culture.

The Maya built large cities. One of the greatest was Tikal (tee-KAL), which thrived for

Ruins of the ancient Maya city of Tikal, in what is now Guatemala

more than one thousand years. The Maya constructed many buildings, temples, and pyramids at Tikal to honor their leaders and the gods.

It took thousands of Maya men to build a temple. The rocks they used were huge. Some weighed many tons. The Maya had no animals such as horses, oxen, or donkeys to carry the building materials. All the work was done by human power and without the aid of the wheel.

Chichén Itzá was one of the largest Maya cities.

As in other Maya cities, Tikal's temples and important religious buildings were located

15

in the center of the city. The village homes and farmlands were outside the center.

Palenque (pa-LEN-kay), Copan (co-PON), Chichén Itzá (chee-CHEN eet-SA) and Yaxchilán (YASH-chee-lan) were other important Maya cities. Today, some of these cities' great temples and art-work have been uncovered. They show how skilled and powerful the Maya were.

The tomb at the Temple of Inscriptions at Palenque (above) is that of a great Maya king. Scribes recorded the accomplishments of their kings on tall rocks called *stele* (right). This stele is at Copan, in what is today Honduras.

Daily Life

Daily life for the average Maya person was difficult. Maya women were responsible for the household and the children. They prepared all the food. The women also made the fabric used for clothing. They wove strong and beautiful cloth.

Like Maya women today, ancient Maya women ground maize on a stone called a *metate* (top left) and then formed the dough into tortillas (top right). Maya houses have been built the same way for more than a thousand years (left).

Maya farmers still practice the ancient slash-and-burn method of farming.

Maya men were skilled farmers. Their main crop was maize, a type of corn. They used a farming method called "slash and burn." During the dry season, they cut down all the plants in one patch of the forest. After letting the plants dry out, they burned them and turned them into ash. Then they planted seeds in the ground under the ash.

When the rains came, it washed the ash into the soil and made the soil richer. The crops did very well this way, but the burned ground stayed **fertile** for only a few years. Then the people had to start the process again in a new part of the rain forest.

Terraced farmland in Guatemala today

In hilly regions, Maya farmers **terraced** the land for farming. That way, the plants could grow on a level surface and be watered without the water running downhill.

The Maya used cacao (Ka-KAW) beans as money. Chocolate is made from these beans. Cacao beans were very valuable to the Maya. Only wealthy people could afford to eat chocolate. The Maya drank the chocolate in liquid form. Liquid chocolate was believed to contain great powers.

Cacao beans were so valuable to the Maya that they were used as money.

To the ancient Maya, large noses and flat foreheads were beautiful.

Like all cultures, the ancient Maya had their own ideas about beauty. They thought flat fore-heads were beautiful. They gave their children flatter foreheads by binding boards to their heads as infants. The Maya knew that an infant's skull is soft and can be shaped easily. The flat board stayed in place on the baby until the skull had flattened and hardened.

The Maya also thought large noses were beautiful. To make their noses bigger, they sometimes put clay on top of them. Shaped teeth were another sign of beauty in the ancient Maya world. Some people filed their front teeth into sharp points.

Ancient Maya Beliefs

The Maya believed in many gods, including a sun god, a moon god, a rain god, and a god of the maize.

Perhaps one of the most important tasks of Maya kings was leading religious ceremonies to honor these gods. These ceremonies often

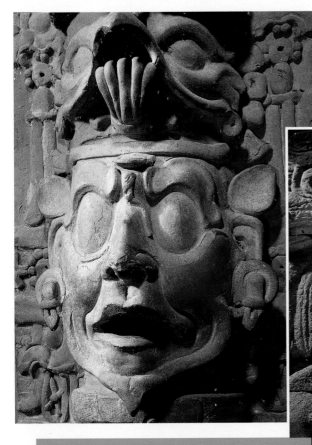

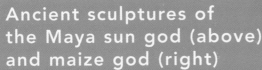

Ancient sculptures of
the Maya sun god (above)
and maize god (right)

included giving something to
the gods, such as precious
jade or **incense**.

Jade

The ancient Maya prized a type of stone called jade more than any other material. The Maya traded goods with people living to the south for jade. They carved these stones and used them in ceremonies. Jade items were sometimes offered to the gods or buried with Maya kings when they died.

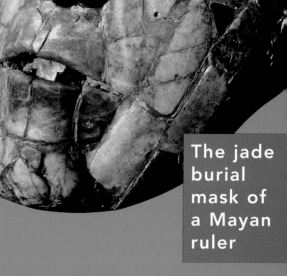

The jade burial mask of a Mayan ruler

The most important cere-
monies included offerings of
blood. The Maya believed that
blood was **sacred.** They thought
offering it would bring them the

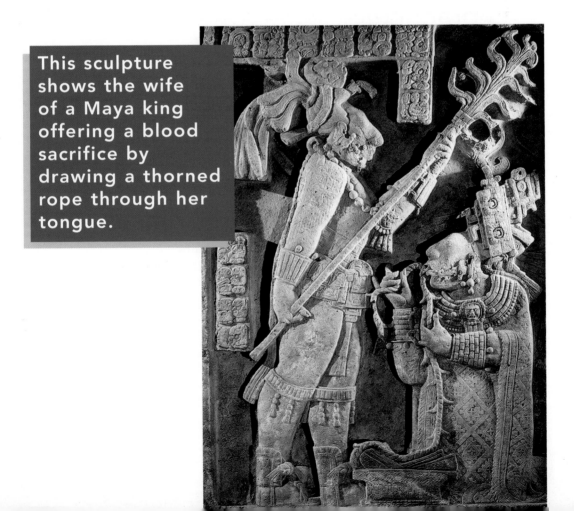

This sculpture
shows the wife
of a Maya king
offering a blood
sacrifice by
drawing a thorned
rope through her
tongue.

help of the gods. Sometimes, Maya kings offered their own blood to the gods. This was a dangerous and painful practice.

The Maya also honored their gods by playing a sacred ball game. The object of the game was to hit a heavy rubber ball through the stone rings high up on the sides of the court. Players could touch the ball only with their shoulders, chest, and

The Great Ball Court
at Chichén Itzá

hips. Losing the game was a
bad idea. Losers were often
beheaded or became the
slaves of the winners.

Europeans Arrive

By A.D. 900, the great city of Tikal was **abandoned**. Other cities in the southern Maya region were left empty as well. No one knows why the people left or exactly where they went.

Meanwhile, the northern Maya cities continued to do well. However, there were frequent

After the Maya left Tikal, the jungle grew up around it. Eventually, Tikal and other abandoned Maya cities were forgotten.

changes in power. By A.D. 1200, many of these cities were abandoned, too. Before long, plants and soil covered the Maya cities. The great temples were forgotten.

Some historians believe the Maya left their cities because constant warring had killed so many people. Others think there were **famines**. With no food to eat, the Maya people would have had to find food elsewhere. Many of the Maya probably moved away from the cities to farm new areas.

In 1502, explorers from Spain reached the ancient Maya homeland. The Spanish came to this new place for two reasons. They wanted to

The Spanish explorers who came to Mexico and Central America in the 1500s mistreated the native peoples who lived there, including the Maya.

spread the Christian religion around the world. They also wanted to get rich from the **natural resources** located in these unexplored places.

The Spanish fought to gain control of the land. They killed many people with their guns and the diseases they carried. The Maya and other groups in this region had never been exposed to these European diseases. They had no way to fight them, and thousands of people died. However, the Maya continued to fight against the Spanish when they could.

The Spanish also destroyed sacred objects and banned the Maya religion. They burned Maya books and tried to erase the Maya culture. Fortunately, the Spanish did not know about

The Spanish destroyed almost all of the Maya hieroglyphic books. This is one of only four known to have survived. These books were made from fig-tree bark that was folded back and forth like an accordion to make pages.

the great temples hidden in the jungles. The ancient Maya cities remained hidden until the 1800s, when American and British explorers rediscovered these amazing ruins.

The Maya Today

For hundreds of years, the Maya people have fought to gain rights and freedom. Even after Mexico and Central American countries declared freedom from Spain, many Maya people were still mistreated. The local governments did not give the Maya people the same respect other people received. In many

places, the Maya were deliberately killed or forced to leave their land. Sadly, even now, this happens from time to time.

Today, about seven million Maya people live in Mexico and Central America. About one million Maya live in the Mexican state of Chiapas. About five million more Maya people live in the countries of Belize, Guatemala, Honduras, and El Salvador.

Today, most of the Maya people live in rural areas and face many problems. These problems include overpopulation, lack of jobs, not having decent health care or education, and the challenge of preserving their culture.

Although life may not be easy, the Maya rely on what they know from their past to survive. They still use ancient farming, building, and weaving methods. Maize is grown much like it was centuries ago. It remains a central part of the Maya diet. Maya homes have been built the same way for hundreds of years.

As with other crafts and skills, the Maya way of weaving has changed little over the last thousand years.

As in the past, the Maya people of today celebrate life through their religious ceremonies. Most of their festivals are a blend of Christian and ancient Maya traditions. Ancient Maya objects and dances are a major part of these ceremonies.

One of the largest Maya festivals takes place in Mexico. It is the Festival of Games, which lasts for five days. Women weave and then wear *huipiles* (we-pee-lace) to the festival. A huipile is a style of woven

Festivals are among the many ways the Maya celebrate their past, their present, and their future.

blouse that the Maya women have worn for centuries. Into their fabric, the women weave the ancient designs and symbols of their ancestors. The patterns and colors tell of a long and impressive history.

To Find Out More

Here are some additional resources to help you learn more about the Maya:

 **Books**

Chrisp, Peter. **The Maya.** Raintree/Steck Vaughn, 1999.

Lourie, Peter. **The Mystery of the Maya: Uncovering the Lost City of Palenque.** Boyd Mills, 2001.

Mann, Elizabeth. **Tikal: The Center of the Maya World** (Wonders of the World). Mikaya Press, 2002.

Nicholson, Robert. **The Maya.** Chelsea House, 1994.

Staub, Frank. **The Children of the Yucatán** (The World's Children). Carolrhoda Books, 1996.

Organizations and Online Sites

Chichén Itzá
http://www.facultysenate. villanova.edu/maya/itza. html

This site, from Villanova University, has many excellent pictures of Chichén Itzá.

Maya Civilization
http://www.civilization.ca/ civil/maya/mmc09eng.html

This interesting site gives a detailed timeline of the Maya culture.

Maya Language
http://www.kstrom.net/isk/ maya/mayatab1.html

This fun site lists common Maya phrases and includes pronunciations so you can practice saying Maya words.

Mayan Kids Interactive
http://mayankids.com/ mkintro.htm

This site has lots of fascinating facts about the history, people, places, beliefs, and games of the Maya.

Mystery of the Maya
http://www.civilization.ca/ civil/maya/mmp05eng.html

A visit to this site will show you an archaeological dig!

The Tikal National Park, Peten, Guatemala
http://www.global-travel. co.uk/tikal1.htm

This travel site has excellent photographs of the ancient Maya city of Tikal.

Important Words

abandoned deserted; left behind

astronomers people who study the stars and planets

beheaded to have had one's head cut off

civilization society that has a high level of culture, industry, and science

culture group of people and their customs

famine widespread lack of food that causes people to starve

fertile able to produce good crops

incense substance that gives off a pleasing odor when burned

natural resources sources of raw material, power, or wealth provided by nature

sacred having religious importance

sacrificed killed as an offering to the gods

terraced formed land into step-like levels